Building Spanish Vocabulary

By Cynthia Downs

Cover Design by
Christian Olsen

Illustrations by
Shauna Mooney Kawasaki

Carson-Dellosa Publishing Company, Inc.
Greensboro, North Carolina

Credits

Author: Cynthia Downs
Artist: Shauna Mooney Kawasaki
Cover Art Direction: Annette Hollister-Papp
Cover Design: Christian Olsen
Cover Photographs: © Comstock, Inc. and © Photodisc
Spanish Consultants: Jessica Orme-Cabo and Miguel Cabo-Busnadiego
Editor: Kelly Morris Huxmann
Graphic Design and Layout: Mark Conrad

ISBN: 0-88724-918-3

Table of Contents

How to Use This Book

Welcome to *Building Spanish Vocabulary*! This book is designed to help you introduce Spanish into the classroom, emphasizing vocabulary development. Easy-to-use worksheets and activity ideas provide fun and simple ways to practice Spanish. And the guide on page 5 helps outline proper Spanish pronunciation.

This book includes vocabulary cards for 360 different words. But these lists are not exhaustive, so add to the vocabulary cards by making your own. Use the vocabulary card pattern on page 6 to make cards in Spanish, English, or both languages. Incorporate your new word cards into the activities described throughout this book.

To help keep your cards organized, copy each set onto a different color paper. This will make it easy to clean up at the end of the day.

There are lots of practical ways to use the vocabulary cards. Here are just a few ideas:
- ◆ Play charades. Break students into teams. One student chooses a vocabulary card and must act out the word. The first team to guess the Spanish word wins a point.
- ◆ Give students a certain number of word cards. Students must create a sentence with the card or cards. Continue with other students to create a story.
- ◆ Use the cards as flash cards. Have students work in pairs. One student holds up a card, and the other must give the translation, singular or plural form, or use the word in a sentence. Have students switch roles.
- ◆ Have students choose a vocabulary card and then place the card on the object named or on a picture of the object. For some vocabulary, pointing may also work.
- ◆ Play a game of old maid where students match Spanish and English word cards for a pair. Remove one word card and deal the rest to the players. Players put down any matches they have, then take turns choosing one card from the player on the right. The object of the game is to play all your cards. If the player left holding a card can name the match, everyone wins the game.
- ◆ Divide students into two teams. The game leader chooses a vocabulary card and shows it to one member of each team. Those two people have to draw the object or concept as their teams try to guess the word.

Here are other fun ways to practice vocabulary:
- ◆ Give each student a copy of the bingo board on page 7. Have students choose from a given list of vocabulary and write one word in each space. Choose someone to call out the words in Spanish or in English (the opposite of what the students wrote on their boards). The first player to get five words in a row shouts "Bingo!" to win the game.
- ◆ Have students name as many Spanish words in a specific category as they can in one minute. Examples of categories: pieces of furniture, animals, articles of clothing, words that begin with "d," and so on.
- ◆ Have students form a circle and count forwards, count backwards, or skip count.
- ◆ Hold a Spanish spelling bee.
- ◆ Have students look at a scene, then flip it over. How many Spanish words can they list that were shown in the picture?

Pronunciation Guide

Use this chart to practice proper pronunciation of Spanish words.

Letter	Spanish Example	Spanish Word for Letter	Sound in English
a	agua	a	octopus
b	bebé	be	boat
c *	cepillo or coco	ce	celery or cola
ch **	chocolate	che	chess
d	dedo	de	dog
e	elefante	e	rake
f	fuego	efe	family
g *	gato or gigante	ge	gate or hill
h	hoja	hache	hour (silent)
i	isla	i	meat
j	jirafa	jota	hot
k	koala	ka	kangaroo
l	limón	ele	listen
ll **	llanta	elle	yawn
m	manzana	eme	map
n	número	ene	number
ñ	ñu	eñe	canyon
o	ocho	o	open
p	papalote	pe	potato
q	queso	cu	cool
r	rama	ere	rat
rr ***	perro	erre	Robert (roll the r)
s	siete	ese	sun
t	tigre	te	tan
u	uvas	u	balloon
v	violín	ve	baby
w	wafle	doble ve	worm
x	xilófono	equis	xylophone
y	yate	i griega	yellow
z	zorro	zeta	set

* The letters c and g are pronounced differently, depending on the vowel that follows. A c followed by a, o, or u would be pronounced like the k in "kite." A c followed by an i or e is pronounced like the s in "simple." Similarly, a g followed by an a, o, or u would be pronounced like the g in "goat." A g followed by an i or e is pronounced like the h in "hill."

** The letter combinations ch and ll are traditionally considered unique letters in the Spanish alphabet.

*** The letter combination rr is not always considered a separate letter, but it is a unique sound in Spanish.

		Libre		

Un plano de la clase

A Classroom Map

Draw a map of your classroom in the space below. Include and label these items:

la silla ....chair
el pizarrón ....chalkboard
la puerta ....door
el reloj ....clock
la tiza ....chalk
la bandera ....flag

el pupitre ....desk
la ventana.....................window
el pared.........................wall
el sacapuntas ....pencil sharpener
el borrador ....eraser
la mesa..........................table

En mi mochila
In My Backpack

Cut out the cards at the bottom of the page.
Glue the things you might take to school with you onto the picture of the backpack.

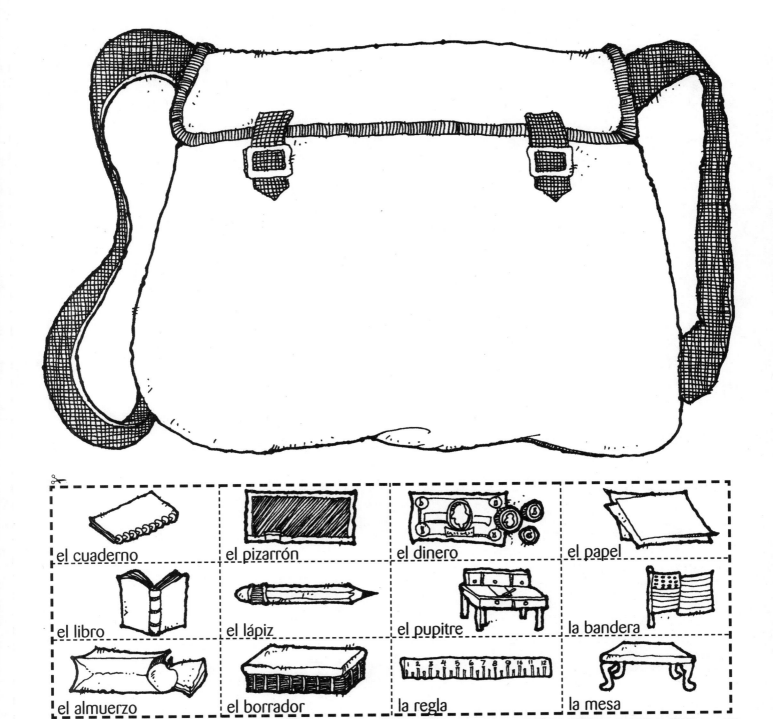

el cuaderno

el pizarrón

el dinero

el papel

el libro

el lápiz

el pupitre

la bandera

el almuerzo

el borrador

la regla

la mesa

CD-4340 *Building Spanish Vocabulary*

Busque a su alrededor

Look Around

Look around your classroom. You will find more than one of many objects. Remember three simple rules to form the plural of a noun:

- ◆ If a word ends in a vowel, add "**s**."
- ◆ If a word ends in a consonant, add "**es**."
- ◆ If a word ends in "**z**," change the z to c and add "**es**."

Use these rules to write the singular or plural form of each word.

Singular	Plural
1. silla	_____
2. pupitre	_____
3. borrador	_____
4. _____	ventanas
5. _____	puertas
6. pared	_____
7. cuaderno	_____
8. _____	plumas
9. _____	mochilas
10. lápiz	_____
11. libro	_____
12. papel	_____

Mi clase
My Classroom

Name: _____

Fill in the blocks with the correct letters to form each word below.
Then write the letter of the matching picture on the line.

libro	pupitre	piso	tijeras	tiza
papel	bandera	ventana	bolígrafo	mochila

1. 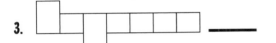 _____

2. 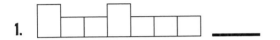 _____

3. 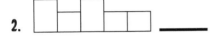 _____

4.  _____

5.  _____

6. 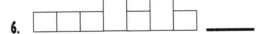 _____

7.  _____

8. 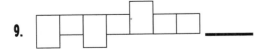 _____

9. _____

10.  _____

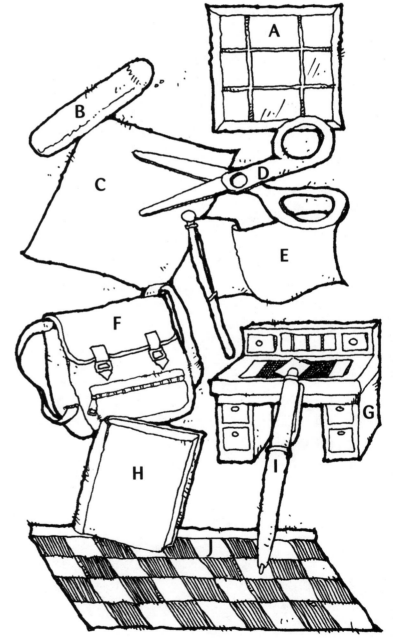

CD-4340 *Building Spanish Vocabulary*

Un cuento en "Spanglish"

A Spanglish Story

Name: _____

Listen to the Spanish words you hear in the story. Can you tell what they mean?
Find the English meanings for the Spanish words below. Write the correct letter on each line.

Mi clase

La puerta opened and all the estudiantes entered la sala. I was scared. I couldn't find mi pupitre. I asked el maestro, ¿Dónde está mi pupitre? El maestro said, Está next to el pizarrón, near la ventana. "I see it. It has mi nombre on it." I put mi mochila on the back of mi silla. I put mis libros, lápices, papeles, and bolígrafo on la mesa under la ventana. I opened mi cuaderno and put mi tarea in the basket by la pared.

1. la puerta _____
2. estudiantes _____
3. la sala _____
4. mi pupitre _____
5. el maestro _____
6. dónde está _____
7. está _____
8. el pizarrón _____
9. la ventana _____
10. mi nombre _____
11. mi mochila _____
12. mi silla _____
13. mis libros _____
14. lápices _____
15. papeles _____
16. bolígrafo _____
17. la mesa _____
18. mi cuaderno _____
19. mi tarea _____
20. la pared _____

A. my chair
B. pencils
C. my backpack
D. pen
E. table
F. students
G. papers
H. my notebook
I. the door
J. my homework
K. the classroom
L. the window
M. the wall
N. where is
O. it is
P. the teacher
Q. my desk
R. the chalkboard
S. my name
T. my books

la silla	el pupitre
el pizarrón	la tiza
la puerta	la pared
la ventana	el sacapuntas
la mesa	la bandera
el borrador	el reloj

desk	chair
chalk	chalkboard
wall	door
pencil sharpener	window
flag	table
clock	eraser

CD-4340 *Building Spanish Vocabulary*

el cuaderno	la tarea
el lápiz	el bolígrafo
las tijeras	la regla
el papel	el/la estudiante
la mochila	el maestro/ la maestra
el libro	el almuerzo

homework	notebook
pen	pencil
ruler	scissors
student	paper
teacher	backpack
lunch	book

Los números

Numbers

Name: _____

Can you count to 20 in Spanish? Count aloud as you write each number.

0	cero	_____
1	uno	_____
2	dos	_____
3	tres	_____
4	cuatro	_____
5	cinco	_____
6	seis	_____
7	siete	_____
8	ocho	_____
9	nueve	_____
10	diez	_____
11	once	_____
12	doce	_____
13	trece	_____
14	catorce	_____
15	quince	_____
16	dieciséis	_____
17	diecisiete	_____
18	dieciocho	_____
19	diecinueve	_____
20	veinte	_____

CD-4340 *Building Spanish Vocabulary*

Write the Spanish number words on the lines.

21	veintiuno	27	veintisiete	60	sesenta
22	veintidós	28	veintiocho	70	setenta
23	veintitrés	29	veintinueve	80	ochenta
24	veinticuatro	30	treinta	90	noventa
25	veinticinco	40	cuarenta	100	cien (ciento)
26	veintiséis	50	cincuenta	1.000	mil

A. twenty-one _____

B. twenty-two _____

C. twenty-three _____

D. twenty-four _____

E. twenty-five _____

F. twenty-six _____

G. twenty-seven _____

H. twenty-eight _____

I. twenty-nine _____

J. thirty _____

K. forty _____

L. fifty _____

M. sixty _____

N. seventy _____

O. eighty _____

P. ninety _____

Q. hundred _____

R. thousand _____

Los números

Numbers

Fill in the Spanish words for the numbers 0 to 12.

0	cero
1	uno
2	dos
3	tres
4	cuatro
5	cinco
6	seis
7	siete
8	ocho
9	nueve
10	diez
11	once
12	doce

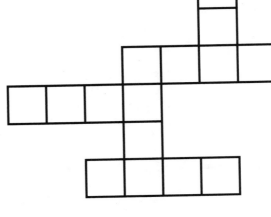

CD-4340 *Building Spanish Vocabulary*

Cut pages 20–22 along the dashed lines. Count the apples in the tree
and fill in the number on each page. Color the pictures and staple the pages in order.

Diez manzanas en el árbol

Ten Apples in the Tree

Diez manzanas en el árbol.
Una se cae,
entonces hay _____.

Ten apples in the tree.
One falls and then there are _____.

1

Nueve manzanas en el árbol.
Una se cae,
entonces hay _____.

Nine apples in the tree.
One falls and then there are _____.

2

Ocho manzanas en el árbol.
Una se cae,
entonces hay _____.

Eight apples in the tree.
One falls and then there are _____.

3

CD-4340 *Building Spanish Vocabulary*

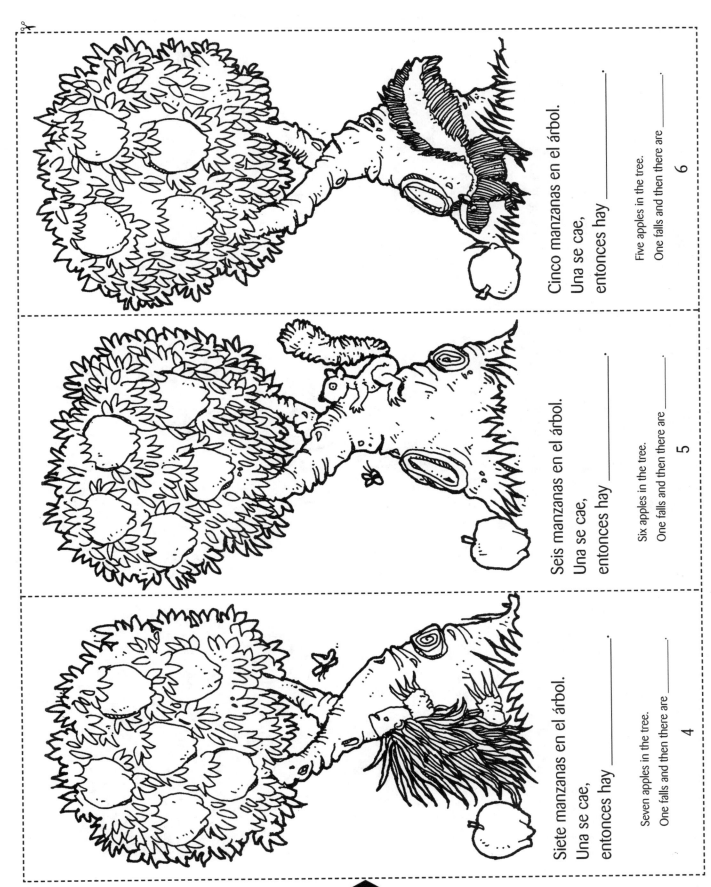

Cinco manzanas en el árbol.
Una se cae,
entonces hay _____.

Five apples in the tree.
One falls and then there are _____.

6

Seis manzanas en el árbol.
Una se cae,
entonces hay _____.

Six apples in the tree.
One falls and then there are _____.

5

Siete manzanas en el árbol.
Una se cae,
entonces hay _____.

Seven apples in the tree.
One falls and then there are _____.

4

Cuatro manzanas en el árbol.
Una se cae,
entonces hay _____
_____.

Four apples in the tree.
One falls and then there are
_____.

7

Tres manzanas en el árbol.
Una se cae,
entonces hay _____
_____.

Three apples in the tree.
One falls and then there are
_____.

8

Dos manzanas en el árbol.
Una para ti y una para mi.
¡No hay más manzanas!

Two apples in the tree.
One for you and one for me.
No more apples!

9

El calendario

The Calendar

The calendar is an ideal tool for practicing Spanish. You can use it to teach counting, months of the year, days of the week, dates, and more. Incorporate the calendar into your daily Spanish routine. The repetition will help students get a firm grip on these concepts.

1. Create a large monthly calendar for the room with Spanish month and days. Each day, have students recite the day and date. Keep track of special days on this calendar, too. Below is a list of events you may want to highlight.

el cumpleaños de . . .	_____'s birthday
excursión	field trip
día festivo	holiday
asamblea	assembly
prueba	test
estudiante del mes	student of the month
. . . de la semana	. . . of the week
. . . del día	. . . of the day

2. Have students make their own calendars using the pattern on page 24. Encourage them to fill in important school and family dates.

3. Each day, have three students come up to the board. Have one write what today is, one what tomorrow is, and one what yesterday was. Use these phrases respectively:

   Hoy es . . .   **Mañana es . . .**   **Ayer fue . . .**

4. Copy the cards on pages 25–28 and use them as drill cards for vocabulary.

5. Mix up the Spanish month cards. Have students put the months in order and then put the months together next to their respective seasons.

6. Make two copies of the cards. Have students match the English with the Spanish. Mix them altogether and have students find the pairs.

7. Make a copy of the Spanish vocabulary cards and cut them out for a Spanish word wall. How many students can read the whole wall?

Mes: _____

lunes	martes	miércoles	jueves	viernes	sábado	domingo

CD-4340 *Building Spanish Vocabulary*

enero	julio
febrero	agosto
marzo	septiembre
abril	octubre
mayo	noviembre
junio	diciembre

CD-4340 *Building Spanish Vocabulary*

July	January
August	February
September	March
October	April
November	May
December	June

CD-4340 *Building Spanish Vocabulary*

la primavera	el verano
el otoño	el invierno
lunes	martes
miércoles	jueves
viernes	sábado
domingo	el calendario

CD-4340 *Building Spanish Vocabulary*

summer	spring
winter	autumn
Tuesday	Monday
Thursday	Wednesday
Saturday	Friday
calendar	Sunday

Sopa de letras
Word Search

Find the days, months, and seasons in the word search. Circle the words as you find them. Look up, down, left, right, and diagonally.

lunes
martes
miércoles
jueves
viernes
sábado
domingo
otoño
primavera
invierno
verano
enero
febrero
marzo
abril
mayo
junio
julio
agosto
septiembre
octubre
noviembre
diciembre

```
U L Y I R T W U P K M H
D J U L I O H G W Y F K
E H I N F G E O T O Ñ O
M V J F E E L E H P Y E
F A U W M S B G J S U D
J I D R Ñ J Z R U C G I
M H W S X U K B E J L N
I U F E Y N T B V R G V
H G L T X I E W E T O I
M I E R C O L E S U H E
A E T A V Q G R H Y K R
P R I M A V E R A J Ñ N
H B Q U R K G O E U U O
V U M N P W V N R N O W
Q T Ñ A H K E M B D E A
I C E V Y H R L M I T O
L O R B I O A P E C Y G
T D I C C Y N T I I I N
L A G O S T O O T E E I
G G E X J E X T P M F M
P J U E N E R O E B H O
W L O Z A T Z T S R D D
R Ñ S A B A D O X E E K
Y V I E R N E S E Ñ U W
J X N R I Z M A R Z O U P
S F R F L E I R B R P P
K E R B M E I V O N Z H
```

CD-4340 *Building Spanish Vocabulary*

Los colores

Colors

Use the key to color picture.

uno = **rojo**	cuatro = **verde**	ocho = **negro**
dos = **anaranjado**	cinco = **azul**	nueve = **blanco**
tres = **amarillo**	seis = **morado**	diez = **rosado**
	siete = **café**	

¿De qué color es?

What Color Is It?

Write the correct Spanish color word to fit in the boxes. Then color each picture.

amarillo	blanco	rojo
anaranjado	café	rosado
azul	morado	verde
	negro	

1.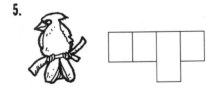

2.

3.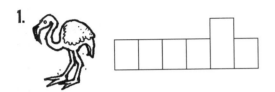

4.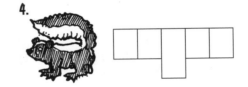

5.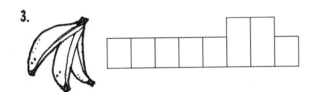

6.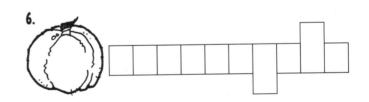

7.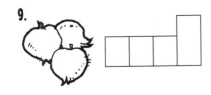

8.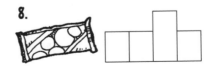

9.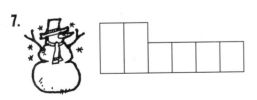

10.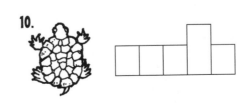

   CD-4340 *Building Spanish Vocabulary*

Las formas
Shapes

 el círculo

 el cuadrado

 el octágono

 la esfera

 el triángulo

 el óvalo

 el cono

 el cilindro

 el rectángulo

 el diamante

 el cubo

la estrella

Circle the object that looks like the given shape.

1. un círculo

2. un cuadrado

3. un rectángulo

4. un triángulo

Write the Spanish word that best describes the shape of each object shown.

 5. _____

6. _____

 7. _____

8. _____

 9. _____

10. _____

amarillo	**morado**
anaranjado	**negro**
azul	**rojo**
blanco	**rosado**
café	**verde**
el color	**la forma**

purple	yellow
black	orange
red	blue
pink	white
green	brown
shape	color

el círculo	la estrella
el óvalo	el cubo
el cuadrado	la esfera
el rectángulo	el cilindro
el triángulo	el cono
el diamante	el octágono

star	circle
cube	oval
sphere	square
cylinder	rectangle
cone	triangle
octagon	diamond

CD-4340 *Building Spanish Vocabulary*

Las formas y los colores

Shapes and Colors

Cross out the letters of the name of each shape. Rearrange the letters that remain to name the mystery color. Write the color name on the line. Then color the shape.

1.

C Í I R R C O M L L U A L A O

_____

2.

C E I R L O I G N D N R O

_____

3.

D O I R A A M D M A N O T E

_____

4.

E R S F D E E V R E A

_____

5.

O Ó R V J A O L O

_____

6.

C A U O A C B D R L A D N O

_____

7.

R C D U O A N A J B A A O N

_____

8.

R E C O T A Á S N D R O G U L O

_____

9.

E L S T U Z R E L A L A

_____

10.

O C É T A C Á G O F N O

_____

Los muebles y la casa
Furniture and the Home

The home is another great context for learning Spanish vocabulary. The topic is familiar to all students and there are a number of activities you can use with this vocabulary. Several ideas are described below.

1. Cut out the home vocabulary cards, mix them up, and have students sort the cards by room.

2. Play an envelope game with the penalty cards found on page 39. Mix together the vocabulary cards and penalty cards and place them in a large 9" x 12" envelope. Players take turns picking a card and then drawing or translating the object or doing what the card tells them to do. When there are no more cards left in the envelope, the player with the most cards in her hand wins the game.

3. Use the home vocabulary cards with any board game. Each player must draw a card and name the picture in order to have a turn.

4. Lay the cards on a table. All players close their eyes while one card is turned over or removed from the table. The player who guesses the missing card first receives a point. Continue playing for several rounds. Vary the game by increasing the number of cards turned over or taken.

5. Divide students into groups of five. Make one copy of the game board on page 40 per student. Each student writes the name of one room at the top of the game board, choosing from **la cocina**, **la sala**, **el comedor**, **el baño**, and **la recámara**. No two students in one group may choose the same room. Copy the Spanish vocabulary cards on pages 41–47. Scatter the cards facedown, leaving out the top eight cards from page 41. Students take turns choosing a card. If the card shows an object found in the room written on the game board, the student keeps the card and places it on the board. The first student to fill his board wins the game.

6. Have each student make a book called "Mi casa ideal." Students should draw each room of the house separately, labeling the furniture and objects found in the room in Spanish.

7. Have students create additional cards for other parts of the house, such as the garage, yard, or basement.

8. Have students create additional vocabulary cards for other items found in their homes.

Cut out the penalty cards along the dashed lines. Mix together with the home vocabulary cards from pages 41–48 and put in a 9" x 12" envelope. Follow the directions on page 38, number 2, to play the game.

Put all of your cards back in the envelope.	**Draw two cards.**
Lose a turn.	**Put two cards back in the envelope.**
Draw again.	**Put something from the kitchen back in the envelope.**
Give a card to the person on your left.	**Lose a turn.**
Take a card from the person on your right.	**Give a card to the person on your right.**

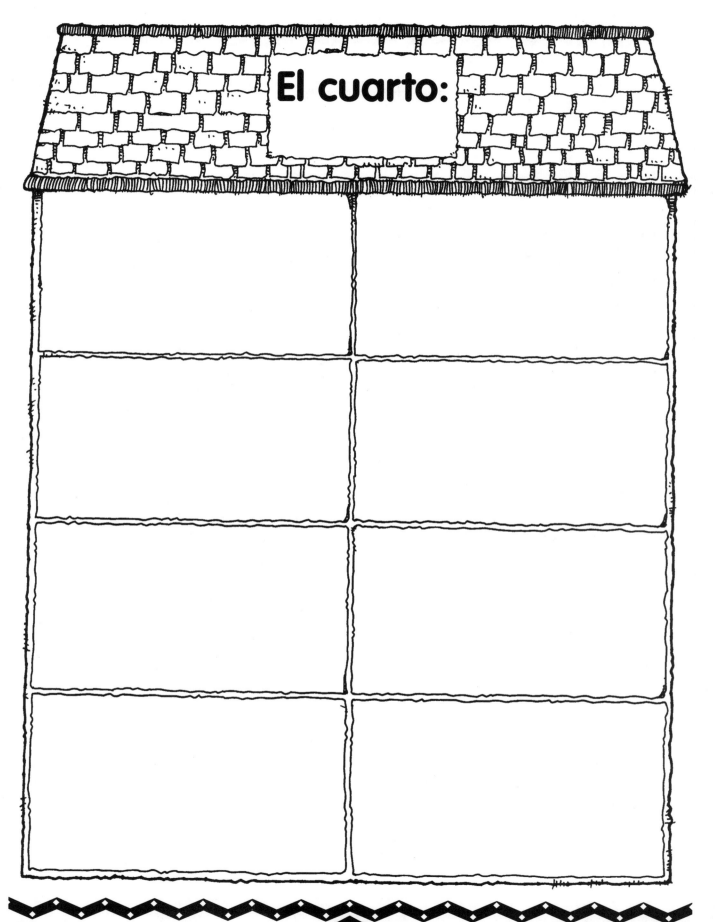

El cuarto:

CD-4340 *Building Spanish Vocabulary*

la casa	el cuarto
el baño	la sala
el comedor	la cocina
la recámara	los muebles
el sofá	el televisor
el sillón	la mesa de centro

room	house/home
living room	bathroom
kitchen	dining room
furniture	bedroom
television	sofa/couch
coffee table	easychair

la lámpara	la mesa
la alfombra	la silla
las cortinas	los trastes
la estantería	la platería
la servilleta	el chinero
el mantel	el florero

table	lamp
chair	rug
dishes	curtains
silverware	bookshelves
china hutch	napkin
vase	tablecloth

CD-4340 *Building Spanish Vocabulary*

la ducha	**la bañera**
el lavamanos	**el wáter**
la toalla	**el espejo**
el jabón	**el papel higiénico**
la cama	**la cómoda**
el ropero	**la almohada**

bathtub	shower
toilet	bathroom sink
mirror	towel
toilet paper	soap
dresser	bed
pillow	closet

 CD-4340 Building Spanish Vocabulary

la mesa de noche	la sábana
el cubrecama	el teléfono
la estufa	el refrigerador
el fregadero	el lavaplatos
el gabinete	el horno de microondas
el tostador	el congelador

sheet	night table
telephone	bedspread
refrigerator	stove
dishwasher	kitchen sink
microwave oven	cabinet
freezer	toaster

La casa

The home

Find the household words in the word find. Circle the words as you find them.
Look up, down, left, right, and diagonally.

sofá	silla	televisor	sala	escalera
florero	cama	bañera	espejo	lavaplatos
sábana	cómoda	baño	toalla	ropero
alfombra	gabinete	recámara	congelador	sillón

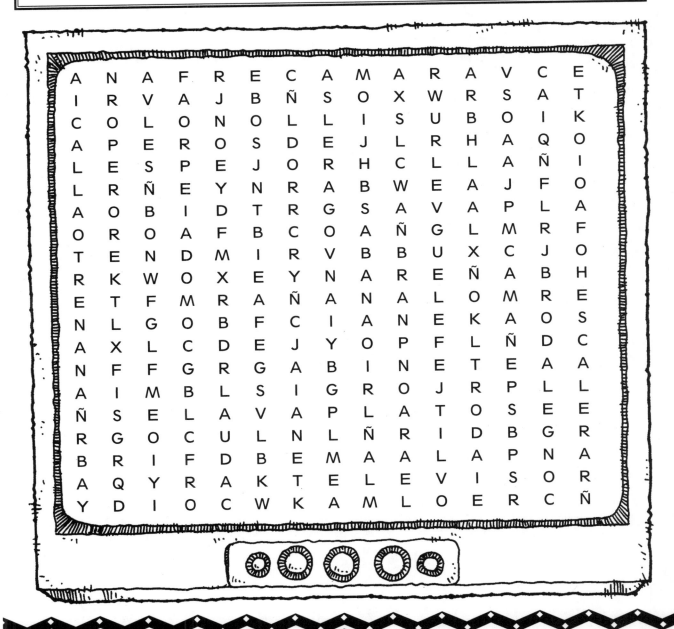

```
A  N  A  F  R  E  C  A  M  A  R  A  V  C  E
I  R  V  A  J  B  Ñ  S  O  X  W  R  S  A  T
C  O  L  O  N  O  L  L  I  S  U  B  O  I  K
A  P  E  R  O  S  D  E  J  L  R  H  A  Q  O
L  E  S  P  E  J  O  R  H  C  L  L  A  Ñ  I
L  R  Ñ  E  Y  N  R  A  B  W  E  A  J  F  O
A  O  B  I  D  T  R  G  S  A  V  A  P  L  A
O  R  O  A  F  B  C  O  A  Ñ  G  L  M  R  F
T  E  N  D  M  I  R  V  B  B  U  X  C  J  O
R  K  W  O  X  E  Y  N  A  R  E  Ñ  A  B  H
E  T  F  M  R  A  Ñ  A  N  A  L  O  M  R  E
N  L  G  O  B  F  C  I  A  N  E  K  A  O  S
A  X  L  C  D  E  J  Y  O  P  F  L  Ñ  D  C
N  F  F  G  R  G  A  B  I  N  E  T  E  A  A
A  I  M  B  L  S  I  G  R  O  J  R  P  L  L
Ñ  S  E  L  A  V  A  P  L  A  T  O  S  E  E
R  G  O  C  U  L  N  L  Ñ  R  I  D  B  G  R
B  R  I  F  D  B  E  M  A  A  L  A  P  N  A
A  Q  Y  R  A  K  T  E  L  E  V  I  S  O  R
Y  D  I  O  C  W  K  A  M  L  O  E  R  C  Ñ
```

CD-4340 *Building Spanish Vocabulary*

En la casa

In the Home

Name: _____

Color the objects that are found in the home.

los trastes = rojo	la platería = amarillo	los muebles = morado

el plato

el sillón

el tazón

el cuchillo

el platillo

el vaso

la silla

el tenedor

la taza

la mesa

la cuchara

la sartén

el sofá

la mecedora

la cama

Write each word under the correct category.

Los trastes (Dishes)	La platería (Silverware)	Los muebles (Furniture)
_____	_____	_____
_____	_____	_____
_____	_____	_____
_____		_____
_____		_____

La naturaleza

Nature

Name: _____

Look at the pictures on this page. Remember their names. Then turn the page over and see if you can identify which pictures are missing on page 52.

el sol   la luna   la nube   la mariposa

el árbol   la rama   la hoja   la flor

el cielo   la tierra   el pasto   la roca

La naturaleza

Nature

Can you name the pictures that are missing? No fair turning back the page or using English!
Write the Spanish word and draw the missing object.

_____   _____

_____

_____   _____

la roca	el árbol
la flor	el pasto
la luna	el sol
la nube	el cielo
la rama	la tierra
la hoja	la mariposa

tree	rock
grass	flower
sun	moon
sky	cloud
ground	branch
butterfly	leaf

CD-4340 *Building Spanish Vocabulary*

¿Cuál es correcto?

Which One Is Correct?

Circle the word that names each picture. Don't be fooled by words you may not know!

Picture	Words	Picture	Words
(clock)	el reloj / la roca	(sun)	el sol / el carro
(clouds)	el televisor / las nubes	(bed)	la rama / la cama
(pencil)	el lápiz / el árbol	(money)	el dinero / el comedor
(triangle)	el camino / el triángulo	(circle)	el nido / el círculo
(chair)	el cielo / la silla	(rock)	la cerca / la roca
(leaf)	la hoja / el libro	(flower)	el árbol / la flor

CD-4340 *Building Spanish Vocabulary*

Las frutas

Fruits

Name: _____

Name the fruits. Write the correct Spanish word to fit in the boxes. Look at the pictures for clues.

toronja	cereza	manzana	plátano	piña	pera
sandía	uvas	fresa	limón	durazno	naranja

1.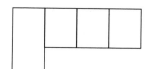

2.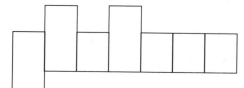

3.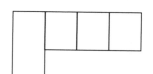

4.

5.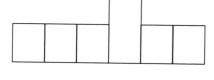

6.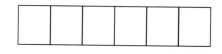

7.

8.

9.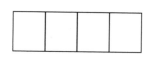

10.

11.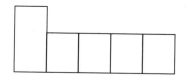

12.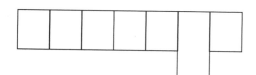

Can you write the English names of the fruits?

La sopa de verduras

Vegetable Soup

Move from one square to the next by writing the vegetable names in Spanish.
Can you make it all the way to the soup?

beans _____

broccoli _____

pepper _____

potato _____

peas _____

lettuce _____

corn _____

onion _____

celery _____

tomato _____

carrot _____

cucumber _____

LLEGADA

SALIDA

Las frutas y verduras

Fruits and Vegetables

Name: _____

Fill in the Spanish fruit and vegetable names to complete the puzzle.

uvas	fresa	sandía	cebolla	toronja	pimiento
piña	limón	pepino	naranja	lechuga	zanahoria
pera	cereza	plátano	durazno	frijoles	

CD-4340 *Building Spanish Vocabulary*

la fresa	el plátano
la manzana	la naranja
el limón	la cereza
el durazno	la toronja
las uvas	la piña
la sandía	la pera

banana	strawberry
orange	apple
cherry	lemon
grapefruit	peach
pineapple	grapes
pear	watermelon

la zanahoria	el tomate
la cebolla	la lechuga
el maíz	la papa
los frijoles	los guisantes
el pimiento	el apio
el brócoli	el pepino

tomato	carrot
lettuce	onion
potato	corn
peas	beans
celery	pepper
cucumber	broccoli

CD-4340 *Building Spanish Vocabulary*

Un juego de memoria
A Memory Game

Cover the bottom half of the page. Look at the top picture carefully for two minutes. Memorize the fruits and vegetables pictured. Then cover the top half of the page and look at the picture on the bottom. Draw and name the missing fruits and vegetables.

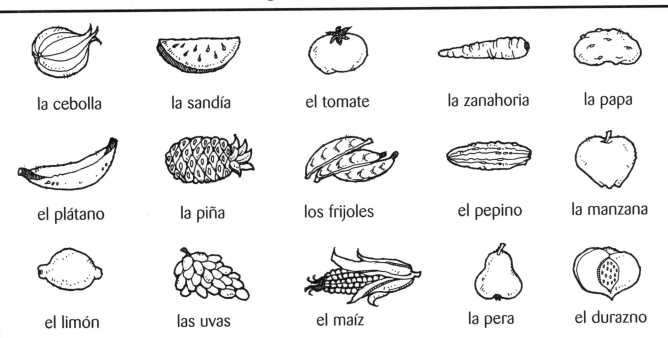

la cebolla   la sandía   el tomate   la zanahoria   la papa

el plátano   la piña   los frijoles   el pepino   la manzana

el limón   las uvas   el maíz   la pera   el durazno

CD-4340 *Building Spanish Vocabulary*

La comida

Food

There are lots of ways to practice food vocabulary. Here are just a few suggestions.

1. Have students sort and match word cards by type of food, color of food, whether the food is eaten raw or cooked, and other categories.

2. Have students make additional vocabulary cards with their favorite foods. Add these to the other cards for use in drills and games.

3. Divide students into groups. Give each group a copy of the menu on page 65. Then ask the students in the group to pretend to order food in a restaurant. Introduce basic vocabulary related to restaurants:

¿Qué le gustaría?...................What would you like?
Me gustaría . . . .I'd like . . .
Por favor................................Please
Gracias ....Thank you
La cuenta, por favor...............Check, please.
¿Cuánto es? ....How much is it?
Su cambio es . . . .Your change is . . .

4. Have students generate their own menus for a special meal, then create a shopping list.

5. Use the game cards on page 66 along with the English fruit and vegetable cards to play a simple game. Have students take turns drawing a card and following the directions. If the card shows a fruit or vegetable and the student can name it in Spanish, he keeps the card. When the envelope is empty, the player with the most cards wins.

El menú
The Menu

Aperitivos

apio y zanahorias
aceitunas
champiñones con ajo

Carnes

jamón
bistec
tocino
puerco
pollo

Mariscos

camarones
langosta
cangrejo
mejillones

Verduras

guisantes
frijoles
maíz
brócoli
col
pepino
papas

Postres

torta
pastel
helado
galletas
queso y fruta

Bebidas

té
café
leche
agua
refresco

Sopa del día

sopa de pollo con verduras

Especialidad del día

paella

Plato especial

pescado con papas

Cut out the game cards below and the English fruit and vegetable cards on pages 60 and 62. Place all the cards in a large 9" x 12" envelope. Follow the directions on page 64, number 5, to play a simple game.

✂

If you draw a food that grows underground, take an extra card.	**No rain! Put 1 card back in the envelope.**
Give 1 card to the person on your right.	**Put all of your cards back in the envelope.**
Draw again.	**Put 3 of your cards back in the envelope.**
Take 1 card from the person on your left.	**Put 2 of your cards back in the envelope.**
Take 1 card from each player.	**Lose a turn.**

el aperitivo	la ensalada
el carne	la verdura/ el vegetal
el jamón	los mariscos
el bistec	el camarón
el puerco	la langosta
el pollo	el pescado

CD-4340 *Building Spanish Vocabulary*

salad	appetizer
vegetable	meat
seafood	ham
shrimp	steak
lobster	pork
fish	chicken

la sopa	la bebida
la pasta	el té
el postre	el café
la torta	la leche
el pastel	el agua
el helado	el refresco

CD-4340 *Building Spanish Vocabulary*

beverage	soup
tea	pasta
coffee	dessert
milk	pie
water	cake
soda pop	ice cream

Los animales

Animals

Look at the animals below. Write each animal's name under the correct category.

el gato   el caballo   la mofeta   la foca

el perro   la ardilla   el mapache   el tiburón

la vaca   el oso   la ballena   el pulpo

Animales domesticados (Tame animals)	**Animales del mar** (Sea animals)	**Animales del bosque** (Forest animals)
_____	_____	_____
_____	_____	_____
_____	_____	_____
_____	_____	_____

Está en la bolsa

It's in the Bag

Look at the pictures. Decide which animal is hiding in each bag. Draw a picture of the entire animal. Then write the animal's Spanish name on the line.

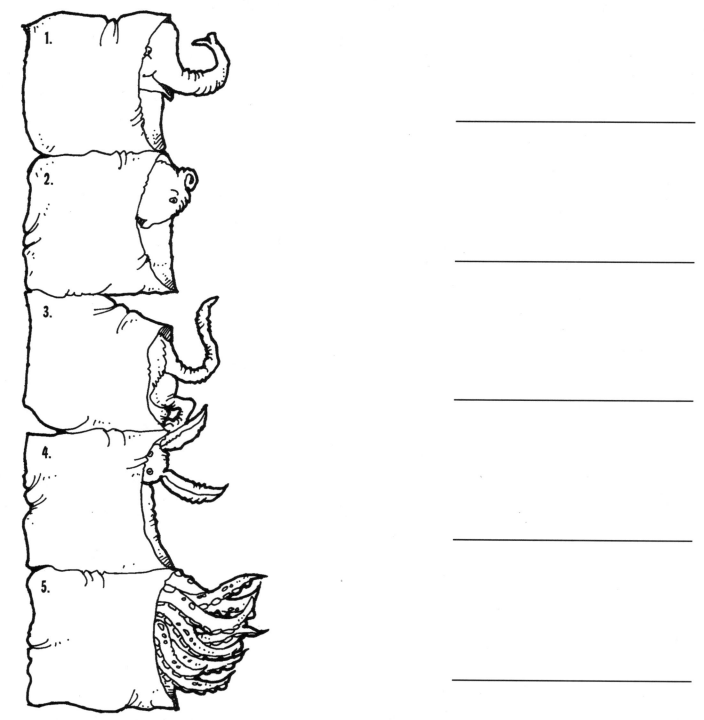

1.

_____

2.

_____

3.

_____

4.

_____

5.

_____

Juego de mesa
Board Game

A board game is a fun way to review vocabulary. To play this game, you will need the game board on pages 74 and 75, one die, and the game pieces below.

Getting Ready:
1. Photocopy the game board and tape the two pages together. Color and laminate as desired. Write one English animal name in each space on the board. (Using a water-based marker allows you to change the board each time you play.) Include animal vocabulary that your students are currently learning.
2. Photocopy, color, and cut out the game pieces. Fold each in half, then fold up along the dotted lines to form the base. Tape as needed just above the base.

Playing the Game:
The object of the game is to be the first one to reach the river. All players start on the space marked "Salida." Each turn, the player rolls the die. Each roll is played as follows:

1–Move back 1 space.
2–Translate the word on the space you are on now. If correct, move ahead 2 spaces. If incorrect, move back 2 spaces.
3–Move ahead 3 spaces.

4–Translate all the words up to the space you are on now. If all are correct, move ahead 5 spaces. If any are incorrect, move back 2 spaces.
5–Lose a turn.
6–Roll again.

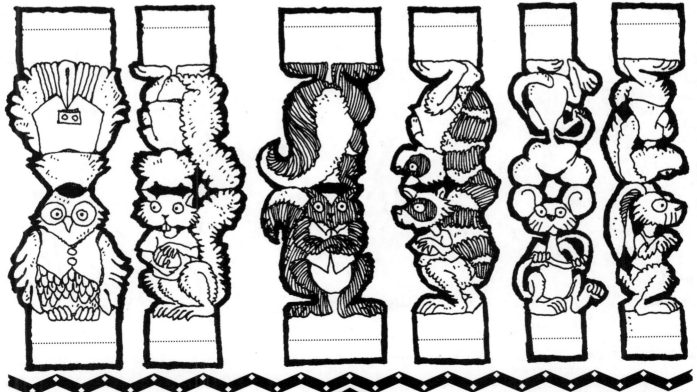

CD-4340 *Building Spanish Vocabulary*

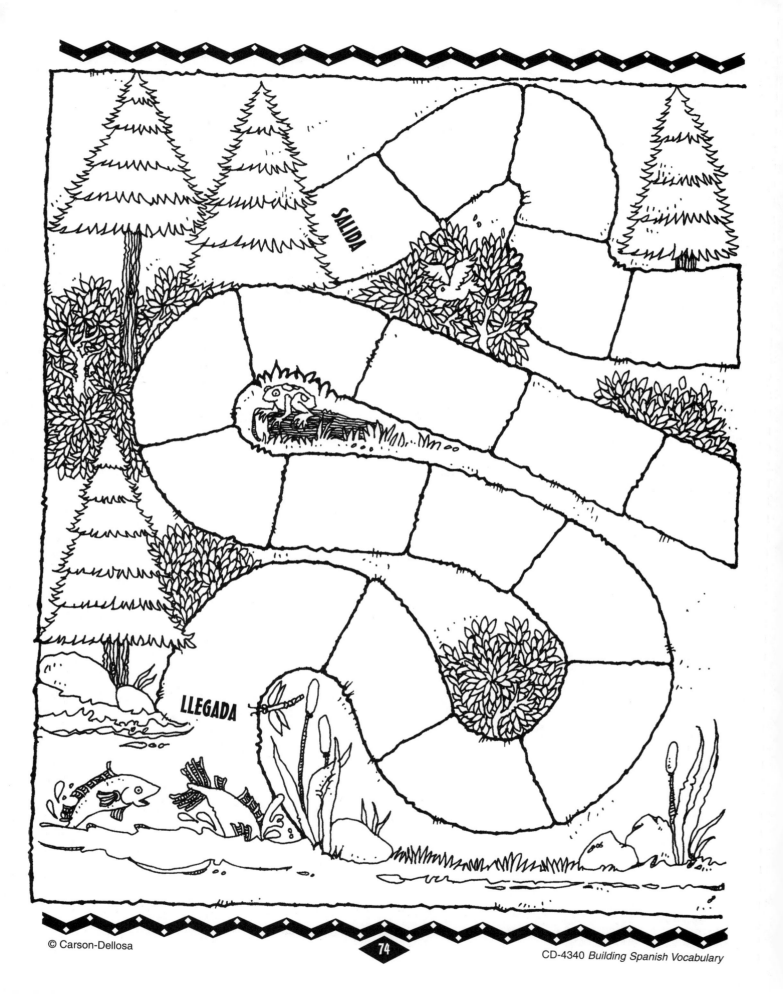

SALIDA

LLEGADA

CD-4340 *Building Spanish Vocabulary*

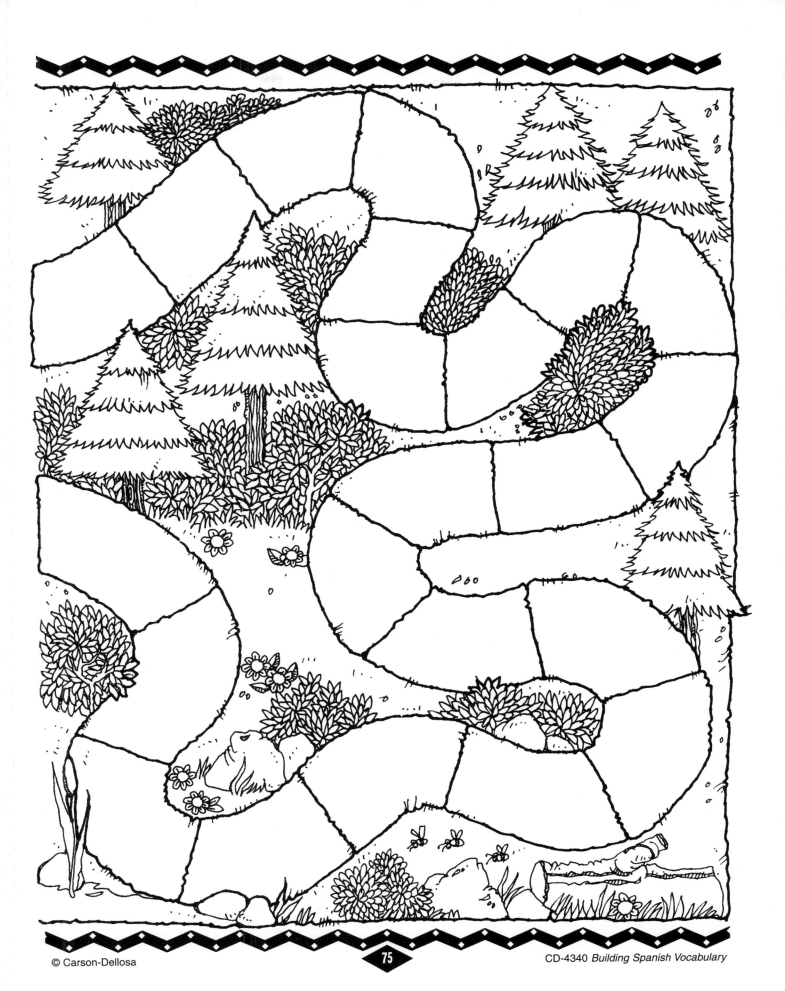

Los animales

Animals

Draw a picture of each animal named.

el mapache	el búho
el pulpo	el elefante
el caballo	el gato
el conejo	el ratón
el pez	el pato

CD-4340 *Building Spanish Vocabulary*

el búho	el conejo
el zorro	el oso
el venado	la víbora
la ardilla	el pájaro
el castor	el ratón
la mofeta	el mapache

rabbit	owl
bear	fox
snake	deer
bird	squirrel
mouse	beaver
raccoon	skunk

CD-4340 *Building Spanish Vocabulary*

el búfalo	**el camello**
el tigre	**el león**
la jirafa	**el elefante**
la cebra	**el rinoceronte**
el gato	**el aligátor**
el perro	**el puerco**

camel	buffalo
lion	tiger
elephant	giraffe
rhinoceros	zebra
alligator	cat
pig	dog

CD-4340 *Building Spanish Vocabulary*

el borrego	la vaca
el pato	la gallina
el caballo	la cabra
el pez	el tiburón
el delfín	el pulpo
la foca	la ballena

CD-4340 *Building Spanish Vocabulary*

cow	sheep
hen	duck
goat	horse
shark	fish
octopus	dolphin
whale	seal

CD-4340 *Building Spanish Vocabulary*

¿Qué no vale?

What Does Not Belong?

Name: _____

Cross out the object that does not belong and explain why.

Example:

La <u>pera</u> no vale
porque no es un <u>mueble</u>.

---

1. El _____ no vale

   porque no es un _____.

2. El _____ no vale

   porque no es una _____.

3. La _____ no vale

   porque no es un _____.

4. El _____ no vale

   porque no es _____.

5. El _____ no vale

   porque no es una _____.

6. El _____ no vale

   porque no es un _____.

CD-4340 *Building Spanish Vocabulary*

¿Dónde está . . . ?

Where Is . . . ?

Name: _____

Look at the picture and the vocabulary.
Read the sentences and fill in the blanks to describe where each thing is.

al lado de sobre	abajo encima de	atrás de dentro de	afuera entre	adelante de a la izquierda	a la derecha adentro

1. El hombre está _____ las frutas.

2. La niña está _____ la mujer.

3. Las toronjas están _____ las manzanas y las naranjas.

4. La mujer está _____.

5. El perro está _____ del gato.

6. Las manzanas están_____ las sandías.

7. Las cerezas están _____ las naranjas.

8. El gato está _____ la sandía.

CD-4340 *Building Spanish Vocabulary*

encima de	abajo
entre	al lado de
adelante de	atrás de
a la izquierda	a la derecha
sobre	dentro de
adentro	afuera

below	above
next to	between
behind	in front of
on the right	on the left
in	on (top of)
outside (outdoors)	inside (indoors)

En la ciudad

In the City

Study the map of the city. Do you recognize the buildings?

la escuela

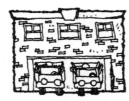
la estación de bomberos

el hospital

el museo

el zoológico

la comisaría de policía

el parque

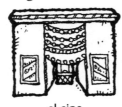
el cine

el mercado

la tienda

Write the name of the building that is located in the place described.

1. al lado del museo _____

2. a la derecha del mercado _____

3. entre el parque y la escuela _____

4. a la izquierda del hospital _____

5. atrás de la tienda _____

6. al lado del parque _____

7. entre el cine y la tienda _____

8. a la derecha del hospital _____

CD-4340 *Building Spanish Vocabulary*

La ciudad

The City

Match the name of each city place with an item associated with it. Draw a line between each pair.

los columpios

la tienda

el cine

la ropa

los animales

el mercado

la oficina de correos

las verduras

las pinturas

el restaurante

el parque

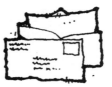

las cartas

los libros

el museo

la biblioteca

las palomitas

el dinero

el zoológico

el banco

el menú

el parque	el zoológico
el museo	la biblioteca
el banco	la tienda
el mercado	la oficina de correos
la escuela	el cine
la casa	el hospital

CD-4340 *Building Spanish Vocabulary*

zoo	park
library	museum
store	bank
post office	market
movie theater	school
hospital	house

la comisaría de policía	la estación de bomberos
el avión	el helicóptero
el barco	el velero
el carro	la lancha
el autobús	el globo
el camión	la bicicleta

fire station	police station
helicopter	airplane
sailboat	boat
motorboat	car
hot-air balloon	bus
bicycle	truck

Transportation

Name: _____

Look at the pictures below. Put them into the correct categories and write the words on the lines.

el helicóptero

la lancha

el globo

el carro

el velero

el camión

el avión

el autobús

el barco

En el aire (In the air)	**En la tierra** (On land)	**En el agua** (In the water)
_____	_____	_____
_____	_____	_____
_____	_____	_____

El transporte

Transportation

Draw a line from each Spanish word to the correct English translation.

el velero	truck
el autobús	ship
el carro	helicopter
el globo	sailboat
el avión	car
el camión	hot-air balloon
la lancha	airplane
el barco	bus
el helicóptero	motorboat

La ropa

Clothing

Find the vocabulary words in the puzzle. Circle each word as you find it.

a. la gorra

b. la chaqueta

c. los mitones

d. los pantalones

e. las botas

f. la bata

g. el camisón

h. el sombrero

i. el traje de baño

j. las sandalias

k. la camisa

l. el chaleco

m. el traje

n. el cinturón

o. los zapatos

```
A T R A J E D E B A Ñ O B A T
X B I N H E M L R O I S P U X
N I C G O R R A D P Q O V T C
S A Ñ A F D Ñ V G A B C D S B
D O W K M E K T O N X E M O A
I R M T D I L C Ñ T F L T E Ñ
X U F B N G S O R A D A J G Y
A J C S R V N A I L S H P K B
T Ñ O B A E J M T O B C O I C
E X V G H E R K D N S G T V A
U D T L Ñ C I O X E M N B H M
Q E K M I T O N E S F D A C I
A G F D S V T Q A G V Ñ T E S
H C I N T U R O N C M O A L O
C B T V S O T A P A Z D B T N
N A S A N D A L I A S A N D O
```

CD-4340 *Building Spanish Vocabulary*

Tiempo para limpiar

Time to Clean

It's time to clean your room! Pick up your clothes and put them in your **cómoda** or **ropero**. Put the toys in your **caja de juguetes**. Write each word under the correct category.

los calzones

los shorts

la falda

el tren

la chaqueta

la muñeca

la camisa

el pijama

el balón de fútbol

el osito

los zapatos

el vestido

los calcetines

el suéter

los carros

El ropero (Closet)	**La cómoda** (Dresser)	**La caja de juguetes** (Toy chest)
_____	_____	_____
_____	_____	_____
_____	_____	_____
_____	_____	_____
_____	_____	_____

la blusa	los pantalones
el vestido	las botas
los calcetines	la falda
los guantes	los mitones
la chaqueta	los zapatos
el suéter	la gorra

pants	blouse
boots	dress
skirt	socks
mittens	gloves
shoes	jacket
cap	sweater

la camisa	los calzones
la bata	el pijama
el cinturón	el traje
el traje de baño	el sombrero
las sandalias	el chaleco
los shorts	el camisón

underwear	shirt
pajamas	bathrobe
suit	belt
hat	swimsuit
vest	sandals
nightgown	shorts

El cuerpo
The Body

Here are some suggestions for using the body vocabulary cards. But don't be limited by these ideas—play around and create your own games!

1. Choose one student to be the leader, switching after a few minutes. All the students stand and the leader reads one vocabulary card at a time. The other students must point to the part of the body named. If a student misses or doesn't know the body part, she must sit down and the next round continues. When there are only a few students left standing, speed up the activity until there is a winner.

2. Have team drills where the students are partnered together. Compare scores or have the winner move to another team until everyone has played together.

3. Have a recess elimination contest. To go out to recess, each student must give the Spanish or English translation of the card read.

4. Play "Simon dice" or "Simon Says." Use the phrase, "Tocate el estómago," for example, or "Simon dice tocate la pierna."

5. Individual practice is always helpful. Eliminate the cards that are not known until there are no cards left. Place a star on a vocabulary chart for those who have mastered the selected vocabulary.

6. Have students alphabetize the vocabulary words, sort them from the top of the body to the bottom, or add them to a personal dictionary.

7. Add the body vocabulary words to the Spanish word wall. For some students, the body parts may be harder to learn if they do not know the names in English. This is a good way to fill in the student's general vocabulary.

Mi cuerpo

My Body

Name: _____

Write the Spanish word for each body part below. Then, find the Spanish words in the puzzle. Cross out each word as you find it.

1. head _____
2. teeth _____
3. hair _____
4. toe _____
5. forehead _____
6. finger _____
7. eye _____
8. thumb _____
9. ear _____
10. shoulder _____
11. cheek _____
12. elbow _____
13. mouth _____
14. knee _____
15. chin _____
16. nose _____
17. neck _____
18. leg _____
19. back _____
20. arm _____
21. ankle _____
22. hand _____
23. foot _____
24. chest _____

```
C  Z  X  V  M  R  Y  K  F  B  A  R  B  I  L  L  A  F
U  H  P  E  L  O  P  A  J  O  C  S  D  L  S  Ñ  U  G
E  K  D  T  A  J  A  M  H  C  U  E  L  L  O  D  O  C
R  R  W  N  T  O  R  E  J  A  E  S  G  A  D  M  J  D
P  D  G  E  A  O  A  J  O  R  F  J  W  B  E  T  A  E
O  Z  A  R  B  X  D  I  E  A  L  R  A  I  D  O  N  D
O  H  D  F  D  L  O  L  O  S  U  R  H  O  M  B  R  O
M  R  I  R  U  Q  S  L  H  O  P  F  S  S  C  I  E  D
A  Z  E  B  A  C  Ñ  A  C  I  N  A  G  R  A  L  I  E
G  F  N  J  W  U  S  X  E  X  A  P  L  O  J  L  P  L
W  W  T  R  A  G  L  U  P  H  R  Y  L  D  K  O  B  P
M  T  E  T  A  N  R  E  D  A  I  Q  U  I  A  G  F  I
G  A  S  E  W  E  I  P  F  D  Z  W  Y  L  O  H  T  E
F  A  N  A  E  L  U  K  G  S  X  E  T  L  P  J  R  A
D  N  O  O  A  T  Y  J  H  A  Z  E  R  A  L  K  E  Z
```

CD-4340 *Building Spanish Vocabulary*

la cabeza	el pelo
la frente	la nariz
la mejilla	la boca
la barbilla	los dientes
el ojo	el cuello
la oreja	el hombro

hair	head
nose	forehead
mouth	cheek
teeth	chin
neck	eye
shoulder	ear (outer)

el pecho	la espalda
el brazo	el codo
la mano	el dedo
la pierna	el pulgar
la rodilla	el pie
el tobillo	el dedo del pie

back	chest
elbow	arm
finger	hand
thumb	leg
foot	knee
toe	ankle

¿Qué es la palabra?

What Is the Word?

Name: _____

Find the correct words to fill the boxes below.
Choose from the vocabulary shown.

cabeza	dientes	ojo	boca	brazo	espalda
codo	tobillo	oreja	barbilla	rodilla	pulgar

1.

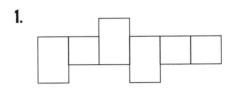

2.

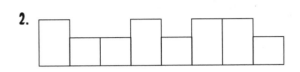

3.

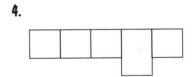

4.

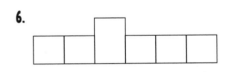

5.

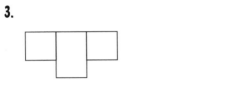

6.

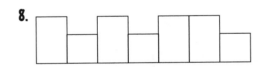

7.

8.

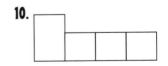

9.

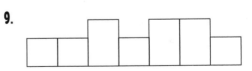

10.

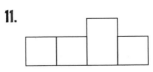

11.

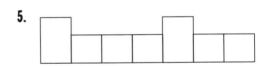

12.

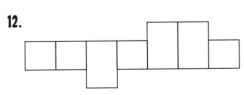

Draw the correct part of the body next to each word.

CD-4340 *Building Spanish Vocabulary*

La familia

The Family

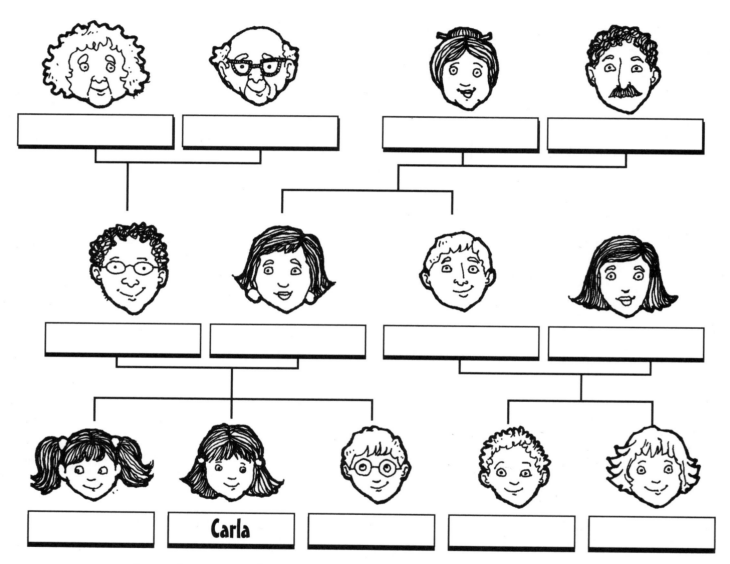

Name: _____

Look at the family tree. Write the correct word next to each family member to show how they are related to Carla.

Carla

la madre ....mother	el hermano ...brother
el padre ....father	la tía ....aunt
la abuela ....grandmother	el tío ....uncle
el abuelo.......grandfather	la prima ....girl cousin
la hermana ...sister	el primo........boy cousin

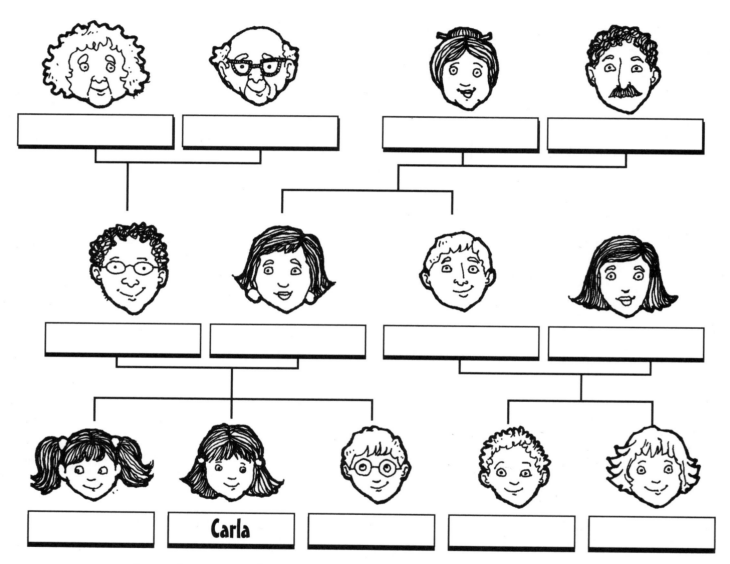

CD-4340 *Building Spanish Vocabulary*

La familia

The Family

Complete the puzzle with the family words below.
Then write the English translation for each word on the line.

hijo _____

hermana _____

madre _____

padre _____

abuela _____

tío _____

hija _____

primo _____

tía _____

prima _____

familia _____

h	i	j	o

Mi familia

My Family

Write the correct word in Spanish to complete each sentence.

1. El padre de mi padre es mi _____.

    The father of my father is my _____.

2. La madre de mi madre es mi _____.

3. La hija de mi abuelo es mi _____.

4. El hijo de mi padre es mi _____.

5. La hermana de mi madre es mi _____.

6. La esposa de mi tío es mi _____.

7. El esposo de mi abuela es mi _____.

8. El hijo de mi tío es mi _____.

Write the correct word in English for each Spanish word.

9. padre _____

10. padres _____

11. abuelo _____

12. primo _____

13. tío _____

14. hijo _____

15. hermana _____

16. abuela _____

17. familia _____

18. hermano _____

19. esposa _____

20. hija _____

The words **mija** and **mijo** are often used by parents to describe their children.

mija = mi + hija   **mijo** = mi + hijo   **padres** = parents

---

CD-4340 *Building Spanish Vocabulary*

la madre	el padre
la abuela	el abuelo
la hermana	el hermano
la prima	el primo
la tía	el tío
la hija	el hijo

father	**mother**
grandfather	**grandmother**
brother	**sister**
boy cousin	**girl cousin**
uncle	**aunt**
son	**daughter**

CD-4340 *Building Spanish Vocabulary*

Los verbos

Verbs

Use your imagination when coming up with ways to practice verb vocabulary. Use some of the general suggestions given at the beginning of this book as well as the ideas below.

1. Play charades with the verb cards. Have one person choose a card and act out the verb shown. The student that guesses the correct verb receives a point and is "it," taking and acting out the next card. Students should raise their hands when they know the answer. If a student calls out the answer, that is considered his turn, the answer is automatically wrong (even if correct), and he is out of that round of play.

2. The leader of this game picks a card and reads the Spanish verb out loud. The others raise their hands and one is chosen. That student has to act out the verb card in front of the class. The others may agree or disagree as to whether the pantomimer is right or wrong. If she is right, she becomes the next leader.

3. Hold a Spanish spelling bee. Have students participate as individuals or in teams. Read aloud a Spanish word and ask the student to spell it. If the student misspells the word he must sit down. The next student or other team then has a chance to spell the word correctly.

4. Independent study is also appropriate. Have the student translate from Spanish to English or from English to Spanish. Have her work with another classmate to add a challenge and valuable feedback.

5. A vocabulary bee can be done in much the same way as the spelling bee, but the task is to translate the words from English to Spanish or from Spanish to English.

6. The Spanish word wall can be a wonderful means of keeping vocabulary accessible at all times. What a wonderful way to compare two languages and to become more fluent in a second language!

Las actividades
Activities

Name: _____

Write the Spanish verb on the line under each picture. Then find the verbs in the word search puzzle. Circle each word as you find it.

_____ _____ _____ _____ _____

_____ _____ _____ _____ _____

_____ _____ _____ _____ _____

```
S H A L R E X Q D P J L T V E R A O G
B L W C R A L I A B K E Ñ O R Q F S I
E Y I N U D C M O T O U Y P W X I J H
B H M M G S A L T A R C F A J H O Z A
D O S B P G I W Z C N A M V X A T E B
I C P Q O I J V U X B H I R E E L P L
B F C E R R A R B I D E W Z Y U A C A
U S A R Y O K R E T P Q B K T I N G R
J V Ñ I L F S O T C U J E E L M U E Z
A K O R A Z B M B A N S Ñ A R O P S I
R R X E B H V T Y N O W U C L T O C B
H A S R R O P I J T D Q R K E H G U V
O T I Z I C A Ñ R A L B C O M E R C Ñ
M R D C R L X B E R K I P W A V S H E
S O I V Y P Q D A T M U H J E Q C A L
U C M O Ñ S R I B I R C S E T I G R D
```

abrir
bailar
beber
cantar
cerrar
comer
cortar
dibujar
escribir
escuchar
hablar
leer
limpiar
saltar
ver

CD-4340 *Building Spanish Vocabulary*

hablar	**comer**
ver	**escribir**
viajar	**leer**
aprender	**hacer**
caminar	**cantar**
correr	**bailar**

CD-4340 *Building Spanish Vocabulary*

to eat	to talk/speak
to write	to see
to read	to travel
to make/do	to learn
to sing	to walk
to dance	to run

abrir	cerrar
escuchar	venir
ir	saltar
mirar	creer
beber	dibujar
limpiar	cortar

to close	to open
to come	to listen (to)
to jump	to go
to believe	to look (at)
to draw	to drink
to cut	to clean

CD-4340 *Building Spanish Vocabulary*

Los verbos

Verbs

Name: _____

Fill in the crossword puzzle with the Spanish verbs below.

ir	cantar
ver	cerrar
leer	saltar
comer	hablar
abrir	viajar
beber	limpiar
creer	dibujar
mirar	escuchar
cortar	

l i m p i a r

CD-4340 *Building Spanish Vocabulary*

Los opuestos

Opposites

Draw lines to match the opposites.

blanco	mojado
grande	fácil
triste	duro
caliente	negro
ligero	débil
claro	lleno
izquierda	adentro
blando	feliz
difícil	pequeño
fuerte	pesado
seco	frío
limpio	sucio
afuera	derecha
vacío	oscuro

CD-4340 *Building Spanish Vocabulary*

grande	pequeño
feliz	triste
fácil	difícil
caliente	frío
claro	oscuro
ligero	pesado

CD-4340 *Building Spanish Vocabulary*

small	**big**
sad	**happy**
difficult	**easy**
cold	**hot**
dark	**light** (color)
heavy	**light** (weight)

CD-4340 *Building Spanish Vocabulary*

izquierda	derecha
vacío	lleno
mojado	seco
limpio	sucio
blando	duro
débil	fuerte

CD-4340 *Building Spanish Vocabulary*

right	left
full	empty
dry	wet
dirty	clean
hard	soft
strong	weak

CD-4340 *Building Spanish Vocabulary*

El monstruo

The Monster

Once upon a time, in a land **atrás del arco iris**, there lived a **monstruo** that loved to count.

He counted
las frutas, las verduras y los animales
in all different colors.

1

El lunes, he counted
diez peras amarillas.

2

El martes, he counted
cinco uvas moradas.

3

El miércoles, he counted
dos zanahorias anaranjadas.

4

El jueves, he counted
ocho tomates rojos.

5

El viernes, he counted
cuatro osos blancos.

6

El sábado, he counted
dieciséis mariposas azules.

7

El domingo, he counted
siete días de la semana.
Then he counted **veinte borregos**
before he finally fell asleep.

8

page 9
Items in the backpack: el cuaderno, el libro, el almuerzo, el lápiz, el dinero, la regla, el papel

page 10
1. sillas	2. pupitres
3. borradores	4. ventana
5. puerta	6. paredes
7. cuadernos	8. pluma
9. mochila	10. lápices
11. libros	12. papeles

page 11
1. bandera, E	2. libro, H
3. tijeras, D	4. bolígrafo, I
5. papel, C	6. mochila, F
7. ventana, A	8. tiza, B
9. pupitre, G	10. piso, J

page 12
1. I	2. F	3. K
4. Q	5. P	6. N
7. O	8. R	9. L
10. S	11. C	12. A
13. T	14. B	15. G
16. D	17. E	18. H
19. J	20. M	

page 18
A. veintiuno	B. veintidós
C. veintitrés	D. veinticuatro
E. veinticinco	F. veintiséis
G. veintisiete	H. veintiocho
I. veintinueve	J. treinta
K. cuarenta	L. cincuenta
M. sesenta	N. setenta
O. ochenta	P. noventa
Q. cien (ciento)	R. mil

page 19
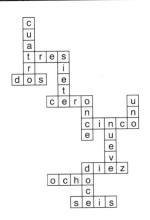

pages 20–22
1—nueve	2—ocho
3—siete	4—seis
5—cinco	6—cuatro
7—tres	8—dos

page 29
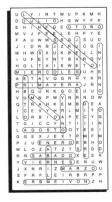

page 30
1 = red	2 = orange	3 = yellow
4 = green	5 = blue	6 = purple
7 = brown	8 = black	9 = white
10 = pink		

page 31
1. rosado	2. morado
3. amarillo	4. negro
5. rojo	6. anaranjado
7. blanco	8. café
9. azul	10. verde

page 32
1. coin	2. window
3. dollar bill	4. pine tree
5. la estrella	6. el círculo
7. el cubo	8. el óvalo
9. el cilindro	10. el cono

page 37
1. círculo/amarillo	2. cilindro/negro
3. diamante/morado	4. esfera/verde
5. óvalo/rojo	6. cuadrado/blanco
7. cubo/anaranjado	8. rectángulo/rosado
9. estrella/azul	10. octágono/café

page 49
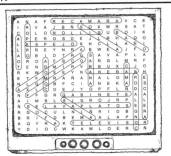

page 50
Los trastes (red): el plato, el tazón, el platillo, el vaso, la taza, la sartén

La platería (yellow): el cuchillo, el tenedor, la cuchara

Los muebles (purple): el sillón, la silla, la mesa, el sofá, la mecedora, la cama

page 52
Row 1: la luna (moon), la mariposa (butterfly)
Row 2: el árbol (tree), la hoja (leaf)
Row 3: la tierra (ground), el pasto (grass)

page 55
el reloj	el sol
las nubes	la cama
el lápiz	el dinero
el triángulo	el círculo
la silla	la roca
la hoja	la flor

page 56
1. pera	2. plátano	3. cereza
4. fresa	5. piña	6. manzana
7. sandía	8. durazno	9. uvas
10. toronja	11. límon	12. naranja

page 57
In order from spoon to bowl:
el pepino, el tomate, la cebolla, la lechuga, la papa, el brócoli, los frijoles, el pimiento, los guisantes, el maíz, el apio, la zanahoria

page 58

page 63
Row 1: la cebolla (onion), la papa (potato)
Row 2: la piña (pineapple), los frijoles (beans)
Row 3: el maíz (corn), la pera (pear)

page 71
Animales domesticados: el gato, el caballo, el perro, la vaca

Animales del mar: la foca, el tiburón, la ballena, el pulpo

Animales del bosque: la mofeta, la ardilla, el mapache, el oso

page 72
1. el elefante	2. el oso
3. el gato/el perro	4. el conejo
5. el pulpo	

page 76
raccoon	owl
octopus	elephant
horse	cat
rabbit	mouse
fish	duck

page 83

1. gato; número	2. tigre; fruta
3. estufa; pájaro	4. lápiz; carne
5. sol; planta	6. árbol; animal

page 84

1. atrás de	2. al lado de
3. entre	4. adentro
5. a la izquierda	6. encima de
7. a la derecha	8. sobre

page 87

1. el hospital	2. la tienda
3. el zoológico	
4. la estación de bomberos	
5. la comisaría de policía	
6. el cine	7. el mercado
8. el museo	

page 88

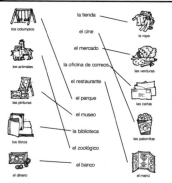

page 93

En el aire: el helicóptero, el globo, el avión
En la tierra: el carro, el autobús, el camión
En el agua: el barco, la lancha, el velero

page 94

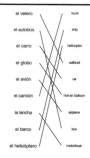

page 95

page 96

El ropero: la falda, la chaqueta, el vestido, los zapatos, la camisa
La cómoda: los calzones, los shorts, el pijama, el suéter, los calcetines
La caja de juguetes: la muñeca, el tren, el balón de fútbol, el osito, los carros

page 102

1. la cabeza	2. los dientes
3. el pelo	4. el dedo del pie
5. la frente	6. el dedo
7. el ojo	8. el pulgar
9. la oreja	10. el hombro
11. la mejilla	12. el codo
13. la boca	14. la rodilla
15. la barbilla	16. la nariz
17. el cuello	18. la pierna
19. la espalda	20. el brazo
21. el tobillo	22. la mano
23. el pie	24. el pecho

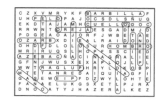

page 107

1. pulgar (thumb)	2. barbilla (chin)
3. ojo (eye)	4. oreja (ear)
5. dientes (teeth)	6. cabeza (head)
7. brazo (arm)	8. tobillo (ankle)
9. rodilla (knee)	10. boca (mouth)
11. codo (elbow)	12. espalda (back)

page 108

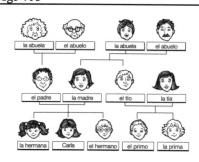

page 109

son
sister
mother
father
grandmother
uncle
daughter
boy cousin
aunt
girl cousin
family

page 110

1. abuelo	2. abuela
3. madre or tía	4. hermano
5. tía	6. tía
7. abuelo	8. primo
9. father	10. parents
11. grandfather	12. cousin (boy)
13. uncle	14. son
15. sister	16. grandmother
17. family	18. brother
19. wife	20. daughter

page 114

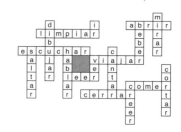

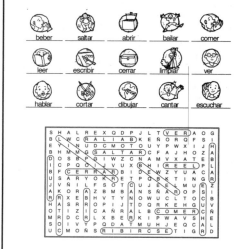

page 119

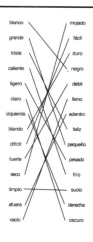

page 120

blanco — mojado
grande — fácil
triste — duro
caliente — negro
ligero — débil
claro — lleno
izquierda — adentro
blando — feliz
difícil — pequeño
fuerte — pesado
seco — frío
limpio — sucio
afuera — derecha
vacío — oscuro

CD-4340 *Building Spanish Vocabulary*